How To Make Money with Your Invention Idea

Brian Fried

Inventor Smart Publishing

Copyright © 2022 by Brian Fried

All rights reserved.

No part of this book may be reproduced or transmitted in any form or by any means, electronic or mechanical, including photocopying, recording or by any information storage and retrieval system, without written permission from the author, except for the inclusion of brief quotations in review.

Published in the United States and the United Kingdom by Inventor Smart Publishing, Melville, NY.

The Inventor Smart name, logo and colophon are the trademarks of Inventor Smart Publishing.

ISBN 978-0-578-29287-8

First edition 2022

Printed in the United States of America

www.inventorsmart.com

Table of Contents

Preface 1

Welcome and Introduction 2
   Why Are You Reading This Book? 2

What Does It Take to be a Successful Inventor? 3

Getting Started with Your Idea 4
   What is Your Invention's Potential? 4
   An Example of Expanding the Window of Opportunity 4
   Evaluating Your Invention's Market Potential 6
   Does Your Invention Exist, or Are There Similar Products That Exist? 7
   Basic Search Tips for Your Invention 9
   Going Deeper with Your Invention Search and Patent Basics 10

Deciding to Move Forward with Your Idea 15
   Name Your Invention & Make It Real 15
   Introduction to Licensing & Manufacturing 18
   What is Licensing and How Do You Earn Royalties? 19
   Manufacturing Your Invention and Starting a Business 22

Take Your Idea Out of Your Head and Make It a Reality 25
   Options to Create a Prototype 25
   Protecting Your Idea: What's a Patent? Why do I Need One? 27
   Tips When Disclosing Your Idea to Others 28
   Can You Protect Your Invention, and What are Your Options? 33

Presenting Your Invention 37
   Get Ready to Pitch Your Invention, and to Whom 37
   Pitching to Direct Response Infomercial Marketers to Earn Royalties 37
   Pitching to Potential Licensees to Earn Royalties 38
   Launch Your Product on Home Shopping Channels 39
   Be Prepared to Pitch 40

Pitching to Catalogs: How Do They Work?............... 40
Pitching To Retail Buyers 41
Understanding Licensing, How to Find and Pitch to Licensees
.... 42
What Does it Take to Manufacture Your Product?.................. 46
Finding A Manufacturer Locally or Overseas to Manufacture Your Product 48
Crowdfunding to Raise Money for Manufacturing 51
Selling to Retailers with One Product 52

Time to Make Money with Your Inventions 54

Understanding Licensees & Licensors, Calculating Royalties and Licensing Agreements 54
Understanding Manufacturing Next Steps 57
Marketing for Licensing and Manufacturing Your Invention/Product.. 61

Congrats on Your Success! Thinking Ahead....................... 65

Preface

At first when you come up with an idea, it can be exciting and yet challenging when you don't know where to go, what to do, and who to trust.

No matter what stage of your invention you're in, *How to Make Money with Your Invention Idea* will help you put your emotions aside and focus on your idea from a business perspective in order to evaluate whether you came up with an idea that will make you money.

This book is dedicated to all the inventors I've had the opportunity to speak to personally or indirectly through the years by one-on-one coaching/consulting, at tradeshows or US Patent & Trademark Office events, public libraries, schools, TV shows, podcasts, and other media outlets, and inventors' clubs around the country.

The most important thing to me is getting the right information out to the inventor community as I share my inventor experience with you, my fellow and future inventors.

You've all been an inspiration for me in writing and making my latest invention happen... this book, *How to Make Money with Your Invention*!

Thank you and keep on inventing!

Brian Fried

Welcome and Introduction

Why Are You Reading This Book?

Hi, I'm Brian Fried and I'm an inventor just like you. Do you have this great idea for an invention in your head? Are you ready to learn how to make money with that invention? This book is about taking action so you can take that great idea out of your head and make smart decisions to help you make money. Here's how it works.

We're going to walk through the steps of getting started with your big idea. We'll also explore how to turn your idea into a real prototype. We'll discover resources to protect your ideas and, of course, help plan your future. As a serial inventor myself, many of my inventions have reached retail where people can buy my products on TV infomercials and home shopping channels, catalogs, and online retailers through licensing and manufacturing. I've also mentored and represented other inventors for 15 plus years at all stages of their inventions, providing feedback and product development, understanding of licensing and manufacturing and also providing turnkey solutions to help make ideas a reality. I've participated as a public speaker at major tradeshows and I continue to lead innovation groups around the country.

So why am I doing this? I want to provide the opportunity for more inventors to learn the process it takes to experience the invention brought to life. Not only to make your invention a reality, but to learn how to earn from your inventions.

I'm honored that you've decided to take this step with me. Now, let's begin.

Brian Fried

What Does It Take to be a Successful Inventor?

Your first thought is probably going to be "great ideas," and you're right. Having an inventive mind is essential. A positive attitude, a willingness to work hard, and a determination to reach your goal are key ingredients also.

But there's something else that every inventor needs if he or she hopes to achieve success. You need the right people around you. You're the boss and you're in control, so remember to make business decisions and separate your emotions. A strong support network, like your friends and family, will help you through the steps to reach your goals. As your mentor I'll help you navigate through your journey, make better decisions, and see your ideas through. So, let's begin by walking you through what you can do now that you have your big idea.

Getting Started with Your Idea

What is Your Invention's Potential?

Who is your idea for? Is it something that everybody can use? For the mass market? Or is your idea for a particular niche? Like for people who play golf or maybe who have trouble walking? I always like to measure and evaluate my window of opportunity when I come up with an idea.

Let's take, for example, a golf ball. Somebody can come to me with this really interesting golf ball that does all types of tips and tricks. When they're at the golf course and look around they may say, "Wow! Everybody in the world plays golf and they're all going to buy my new invention golf ball!"

The inventor becomes really excited about their idea and thinks that everybody's going to buy these golf balls! But when they step off the golf course and talk to people outside of their environment about this golf ball, they may find that not as many people actually play golf as they thought. It's at this point, we have to ask ourselves: Where would my product fit in? Do you think your product is for a niche group of people? Or is your product for the mass market? People will think of your product only in the context of how you tell them to use it. How are you proposing to use your invention in your target audience's mind? If you have to pause here, think about these questions. Where does your invention fit in and how can you expand that window of opportunity for your invention?

An Example of Expanding the Window of Opportunity

I'd like to show you an example of how I expanded my window of opportunity with one of my inventions called "Pull Ties". So, what is it? Well, you push the release button and you slide it up and down the track, and when you let go it stops.

So, why did I come up with it? Well, it started off with bread. Do you know those plastic tabs that come with your bread? They are too difficult to put back on or they snap in half. Sometimes the bread comes with twist-ties that I didn't know which way to open or close. Anyway, maybe you eat bread, maybe you don't eat bread. I had an option of selling to you if you did eat bread, but I said you know what? What if it could be used for other things like, how many times was my cereal bag left open? How annoying is that? I kept realizing that my cereal was getting stale and because the bag was left open. So, now, you take my Pull Ties and you slide it on the cereal bag, push the button release, slide it up, release and seal it tight. Now you can take the outer box of the cereal, throw it away, and you can have a Pull Tie on your cereal bag. And, how about this...

How about in the freezer? Yes. How about those bags and those big family-style bags of French fries and vegetables that you get at the club stores or at the supermarket? You can just take a Pull Tie, slip the open part of the bag in, slide the button up the track and now it seals tight. And how about your chip bag left open? So, what I did was start off with using the Pull Ties for bread. I said, how many people eat bread? Bread, bread, bread. But, right now, I could say how many people eat bread? And how many people can use this in the freezer? And how about finding bags that are open for you to use the Pull Tie in the pantry? How about potato chips? How about your cereal? And some people even mentioned that they used their Pull Ties to keep extension cords, charger wires, and other wires together. So, it started off with bread and then it expanded. Now I can just say how many people have a kitchen? Right? So, that's how you expand your window of opportunity. Think about that for your invention.

Pull Ties continue to sell even after 10 years. They're in retail stores and they've been on QVC, catalogs, and online retailers. It's been a great journey with them. And they'll keep going because there are so many different windows of opportunity and different places that they can be used. Again, think about this example for your invention to expand the possibilities of how and where yours can be used and by how many more people to result in more sales!

Evaluating Your Invention's Market Potential

We left off having you think about whether your idea can relate to more than one industry. Sometimes it's only for one industry and that's okay, but did you think about other industries? Take a moment and think of the different uses and possibilities for your product. You can pause your reading at any time to think about it, write down your notes or possibilities you come up with.

What if you invented a cane that helps elderly people keep their balance? Your product can also be used for people who let's say, have a leg injury or just had leg surgery. That means that you can sell your cane to drug stores, but also to hospital gift shops, to a medical supply company, or even a mass-market retailer. How can you make your invention marketable to more people, open up your window of opportunity, and possibly make more money?

You can experiment and find out that this new way of being used, a new market niche, may be more viable than the one you thought of first, and you would have missed out on that opportunity! When you have a new product, you have to be open to testing. I always like to try new things and here's a lesson I've followed in my life and also as an inventor. I keep what works and I get rid of what doesn't, and then I have more room to keep trying new things and adding more of what works. What do you think?

Before moving on to the next lesson, take a moment to brainstorm your answers to these questions. I challenge you to think of at least three different types of markets, or segments, or types of people that can use your invention. Ask yourself these questions and really make sure to give it thought before you continue:

Who is your invention for?

Is it possible your invention can be used in more than one way? How many different ways can your invention be used?

Where can your invention be sold?

How many types of distribution channels can it be sold through? Does one way have more potential than the other?

Your invention is brand new and nobody has the answer until you try. But it's good to have these thoughts and answers on your mind right now.

Please move on to the next section when you are ready.

Does Your Invention Exist, or Are There Similar Products That Exist?

In the previous section, we spent time brainstorming who your invention is for, who your target audience is, or you may have expanded your target market. Let's take your idea to the next level and begin searching for your invention.

Our goal is to gather as much information as possible and determine if your product already exists. Is there a similar product, but your idea is substantially different? Is your idea just like many others in the market? What should you be looking for when searching for your idea?

First, look for products that are similar to your invention idea. Second, look for products that solve the same problem your invention solves. It doesn't have to be exact, but close enough for you to take a second look at it and keep it in mind as a reference. As you navigate through your search, you'll face one of these scenarios.

Scenario 1: Your idea is unique and entirely new. Congratulations! You've passed the first hurdle, but you're not finished yet. Try to find out why your service or product may not exist or can›t be found that easily by asking yourself and other people from a consumer perspective. Maybe you›re the first with this brilliant idea, but there have been instances when further research has shown that there's not enough demand for your idea in this market or it may be too impractical to use.

Scenario 2: You find a similar product, but your idea is substantially different from others on the market. Well, done! Now, you can take the time to write the comparison between your idea and the product you found. So, this means that you may have uncovered a problem that needs a solution, or you've come up with a better solution. Determine the differences between the product and your idea. Your idea should be unique. See if you can determine what sets your idea apart from the other one.

Scenario 3: Your idea is just like many others already on the market. Don't give up hope though! If someone else is making money with an idea just like yours, it means that you are on the right track! You still may be able to work on it, as long as you're not infringing on somebody else's intellectual property. But if you're going to try to license it, your opportunity may be limited.

Scenario 4: So maybe you hit a brick wall with this idea and the product on the market is exactly the same thing as you were thinking. I sometimes just buy the product and enjoy it and think about the other person or company that just made money off my idea. Well, it's not really my idea because I wasn't the first one.

You've got what it takes to create an invention and it's just a matter of time before you come up with something new. Today's market is immense and there is always room for new inventions and products.

Let's begin our searching options and remember, search to find it, keep your eyes open and your emotions out of your decisions regarding what you find.

Basic Search Tips for Your Invention

What I really like about these initial searches I'm about to discuss with you is that it costs you nothing except your time to explore and to search. Dedicate several hours, it could be for a few days, it could be many days but take your time. It's better to search and find your invention out there as soon as possible than to be down the path of building and investing in an idea that's someone else's. You want it to be your own or enough of a difference to call your own, right? The easiest way to search for your idea is to perform an online search with Google, or Yahoo search engines and check through online retailers like Amazon. I also like looking through AliExpress which is an overseas e-tailer. And there are plenty of other online stores and social media outlets like Pinterest, Instagram, Facebook, and others that have ads running and are selling products when you search for something on their platforms.

Remember, when you put in the words describing your idea in the search bar, it's scouring web pages and finding those words in titles, descriptions, and other tags. Another tip: if you put your phrase to describe your invention in quotes, then it'll only find those exact words together in your search.

Whatever you find, either copy and paste the website or the URL onto a Google or Word doc and capture everything so you can reference it later if you need to compare your idea to what's already out there. When you're searching online, try to use as many different word combinations as possible to describe your idea. So, let's take, for example, if you invented a shoe. You would try specific descriptors like: men's, ladies, children's, sneaker, trainer's, leather, formal, classic, sandal, orthopedic, and so on or just categorize general shoe and footwear.

Now, let's go out and go shopping. Once you've looked online, let's search for your idea in the real physical world. Visit the stores where you envision your product to be sold. Is it a mass- market retailer? Is it a specialty store like a sporting goods store or a beauty store? Which section of the store is your idea in or should it be in? Look around and see if you can find your idea.

Don't forget to grab printed catalogs on your way out and check out many print newspapers that still have advertisements and store inserts, especially in the weekend editions. Just keep your eyes open wherever you are and wherever people are selling things. Now, spend some time becoming familiar with your invention's marketplace. This is time well spent that may help you in unexpected ways. Remember, you're still in the discovery stage. Once you've completed your own research, there's another big step that we need to take. Continue to the next section to learn the steps that may change everything.

Going Deeper with Your Invention Search and Patent Basics

Now that you've determined there's a market for your idea, it's very important that we do some simple patent searching. Doing these searches on your own doesn't cost you any money and it could save you time and wasted effort later.

Many people come to me and say that they have this great idea for an invention. So, I ask them if they've done a search and they say, yes of course! I later found out that their search was only looking down the aisles of Walmart! There is a difference between the research we did in the previous section and the patent search we are going to be doing now.

Here are some patent search tips. You'll also have access to a video showing basics of how to use this information. I recommend searching for patents using the Google Patent Search website (patents.google.com).

Just put in the google search bar, "google patents" and their website results come up. You can click on that link right into that link. And there's also the main site from the U.S. Patent & Trademark Office (uspto.gov).

I think the Google Patents site is really easy to use, but you can use them both. You can begin by using descriptive terms of your idea. For example, if I just came up with a light bulb on top of a pencil, I would type in, "a pencil with LED light," or "pencil that lights up with a fluorescent bulb," or "light bulb attached to graphite pencil," or even look up the same thing using ink ballpoint pens.

Do you get the idea? Use descriptive words. I hear many people say that they're going to search for their idea with this great name or a unique name that they came up with. That most likely is not going to show up in your patent search. So, as you do a search, try to be as clear as possible with your "descriptive" search terms and take your time!

Remember that search results are pulling up descriptions of a gazillion things out there. So, think of the words that would be used to find it! You have to search with your eyes open. I know that it can be very exciting searching for your idea in the patent registry and in all these other searches we've done so far. But many inventors perform these searches with their eyes closed because they're too afraid that they're going to find their invention out there.

The easiest way to start is by looking at the drawings in the patents. Then, you could read the claims listed of utility patents.

Design patents only show the drawings, because they're based on the ornamental design. Utility patents have more to it because those patents describe the functionality of that invention with claims and drawings both included. If you look at the patent number, if there's a D that it starts with, that's a design patent. When you find a patent for a similar idea to yours, you have to determine if your invention will infringe on someone else's patent if you were to continue.

Infringement - it's illegal and it gives the original patent holder the right to sue you if you decide to sell an invention that's protected by their patent. Maybe there is a shot at getting IP, Intellectual Property Protection, if maybe there's a way around it or there's something that is different enough. If your idea is the same as an existing patent, it may be best to just move on to your next idea unless the patent is expired or it's going to be expiring soon. In that case anyone would be able to make it because it's in the public domain as an expired patent. You can produce it and sell it, but you won't be able to get a patent on it.

If you find a patent that's similar to yours, check the expiration date. Design patents last for 15 years and utility patents are good for 20 years. Keep a record of what patents you find and maybe you can reference them for later. If you didn't find your idea or if you have questions about a patent you did find, or if you prefer not to do any of the searches we discussed so far, you may consider hiring a patent attorney or patent agent. I do it all. I check online, I check in the stores, I check in the patent office website and then I still pay for a professional patent search. Remember, when I come up with an idea, I'm starting a business for each one and this searching process is part of my research phase. I would rather know now if I should be working on my idea or if it's somebody else's. The patent attorney, agent or patent search firm you use, are going to be able to go deeper in their searches. This is what they do for a living and they know how to use all the tools and resources from the U.S. Patent & Trademark Office. They can also search through international patents for you. If you want, you can also look through the international patent database by putting in the search engine WIPO, The World Intellectual Property Organization (wipo.int).

The cost of hiring an attorney, agent, or search company varies but you can expect to spend between $500 and $2,000. When you find the attorney, agent, or company that you'll be working with, they'll most likely ask you for details of your invention that they need to search. This includes, a description and some drawings, or maybe if you have a prototype already, you can send them pictures of it or a video or maybe you want to send them the whole prototype. You'll also send them what you compiled, like the similar products that you found in the stores, things you found online that also looked similar and even the basic patent search you started to do yourself.

Once they have completed their search, you can ask them to include a *patentability opinion*. This will provide you with their opinion if your idea is patentable or not when they compare your idea to the other ones that they discovered that might be similar. I have a patent attorney I use and when he gives me an opinion on whether an idea is patentable or not, I trust him. But if I'm not sure about his opinion, I can always reach out to another attorney or agent and get a second opinion. Remember, it's only their opinion and it's going to be up to the U.S. Patent & Trademark Office to ultimately make the decision to grant an issued patent or not. If the patent search comes up and it looks like or has claims like you have, you must decide if you're going to continue to move forward or not. Once I spent 12 hours on my own searching through patents and reading through all these patents out there, and I couldn't find my product. I wanted to still make sure I did a good job, so I gave it to a patent attorney and they found exactly what I was looking for instantly! I spent a couple of hundred dollars paying for a patent search, but I saved time, money, and the heartache of developing an idea that would have been infringing on somebody else's patent.

So, now it's time for you to do your own searching.

Remember, you can just hire a patent attorney, agent, or search firm. Based on what you find, you have to determine, do I move on to my next idea? Or do I move forward with this idea? And what could be my options for licensing to earn royalties or to start my own business? As long as you are not infringing on someone else's intellectual property or there's intellectual property that you could obtain, that could ultimately be your patent.

Deciding to Move Forward with Your Idea

Name Your Invention & Make It Real

Now it's time to make your invention real by giving your invention a name. It makes it easier to talk about and to reference and it makes the process more exciting! When you take the time and effort to name it, you're committing to it in an entirely new way. In many ways, your invention is your baby. It came from you and it deserves a name that fills you with pride.

If you encounter red tape hurdles and possible technical setbacks along the way, the excitement that's fueled by that pride of ownership keeps you focused on your goal. Let's say you invented a reversible all-weather dancing shoe. Do you want to use the phrase, reversible all-weather dancing shoe, every time you talk about it? Suppose you name it using the first letter from each word: R.A.D.S. or R-A-D-S.

That name is much easier to use and when the shoe has a name, it seems more like a real product instead of just a description. You can visualize the packaging and promotional concepts more clearly. It feels more real and you'll feel much more committed to its success also. Even if you love it, the first name you think of may not be the one you end up using as your invention name. You need to search to make sure the name you've come up with isn't already being used for the same purpose as yours.

First, come up with your name, if you haven't already. Once you have a name in mind, search for a domain name just to see if your product name could be available or if it's already taken. Domain names are what users enter online to find a website. Discovering if a domain name is available is a great place to start, because you may be able to buy the name you came up with for your invention. Try registrars like Godaddy.com, which is an easy one to use. Maybe someone has a website up and running or they just have the domain name and nothing is being done with it now or maybe never.

If there is no website that comes up, you can begin by searching whois.net or who.godaddy.com if the domain name is already registered. These sites give you the names and contact information of the people who registered these domain names. The contact information may be public or private. If it›s public, this makes it easier to contact them and find out if they're really committed to the name or if they might be willing to let it go for a nominal fee.

Godaddy.com has a domain broker service for the domains that come up private. Even ,if they're public, they can handle making an offer and trying to capture a domain name you really want, and there may be other options. You can try different extensions besides dot com if that wasn't available like. (dot)net or. (dot) biz or. (dot)info for your domain name. I think .(dot) coms are the best ones to get and those should be your first choice.

Another tip: when searching for your domain name, consider what your "website name" maybe. For example, after searching you find that RADS, rads.com is registered as a "dot com" business by someone who sells radiators. In that case, you might try to make the name more specific like radshoes.com to get around it.

Now let's take a quick trip back to the U.S. Patent & Trademark Office website, uspto.gov.

This time you want to go to the Trademark section (uspto.com/trademarks) and check your proposed name and class of goods to find out if anyone has the name you want. See if there's a filed trademark or a registered trademark that is, the same as the one you are considering using for your invention name.

You may want to consider hiring a trademark or intellectual property attorney to confirm if the name is available so you won't have any issues with conflicting products or services that may be similar. Before you register a name, go through the process at least two more times.

When you've got three names that you really like, it's time to do some informal market research. Run the names you came up with past ten people whose opinions you value and ask them to give you their feedback by listing them in the order they liked the best and telling you why they made those choices. If you feel uncomfortable talking openly about your idea, you can draw up a simple NDA, a Non-Disclosure Agreement, or you can easily find one online.

I have an NDA available on my website, InventorSmart.com, in the footer section that you can download for free. Keep it simple and share only as much information as necessary in order to provide a basic understanding of your concept and the market you think you'll serve. When you approach people to give you their feedback, you need to make it clear that you're looking for their honest reaction. Don't even tell them that it's your invention, so they know that you're not going to take their opinions so personally. People who say kind things to save your feelings aren't helping you in the long run. Choose individuals who understand that you're coming to them for a fresh perspective and that their input has value to you.

Sometimes a casual suggestion to tweak it this way or position in that way can make all the difference when you take your invention to the next level. Once you feel comfortable with your invention and the name you decided on, it's time to make it official. The final step is to register your domain name. You can do this very easily and inexpensively through a domain registry business like

Godaddy.com as I mentioned to you, but feel free to search and compare companies until you find a registrar that suits your budget and needs.

The average cost should be about $8 to $40 per year, and there are plenty of bells and whistles that can be included with them that makes the prices vary. Then, there are also promotional offers you may be able to find for the first year.

We touched on the trademark. You can consider filing as an "intent to use," which means that you would have six months before you would have to show the U.S. Patent & Trademark Office that you started using it in commerce. Otherwise, you would have to keep filing extensions for up to three years or until you actually sell your product. When you start using the name in commerce within a certain class of goods, and you prove it to the trademark office, your ™, trademark, turns into an ® for a registered trademark. Very exciting to name your invention, soon to be a product!

Introduction to Licensing & Manufacturing

You have already accomplished so much! You've discovered that hopefully, you're in the clear and not infringing on another patent or trademark for your invention, you've come up with a name and secured a website address for your future product.

Well done! It's now time to look at your business options when it comes to your invention. I always say it's important that you think about your idea as a business and take the emotions out of the decisions you're going to make. Getting caught up in your feelings can keep you from moving forward with your invention.

You may think you know the path you want to take right now, but your circumstances can change as you move through the steps in this book. Don't worry about making your final business decisions now, we will explore the steps to help you with your options later in the course. However, the decision that you can make now is to figure out the amount of your investment. Investing in your invention requires four elements: *time, money, energy, and effort*. How much of each element do you have available? Spend some time thinking about the amount of time, money, energy, and effort you have to give.

Think about your current situation:

Do you have a full-time job? Do you have a family?

Do you have an active social life?

Take a look at your calendar. How much time and energy are you able to commit to developing your invention or running a business each day or even each week?

Look at your financial situation. Do you have the money to invest in the development of your invention?

Are you ready to learn more about the details and what it takes to have your product distributed into the mass market?

What happens if you find out that you don't have very much of any of these elements? There's no need to feel guilty or give up. Knowing what you're able to invest now helps you to make better business decisions as you move forward. In the following sections, let's look at your business options to get you closer to making money with your invention.

What is Licensing and How Do You Earn Royalties?

Many inventors choose to license their idea because they're limited on funds, or if they have the resources, they don't have the expertise or desire to dive into the many aspects of running a business raising funds, assembling production, developing, and executing a sales and distribution plan, along with other business activities.

So, what is licensing? Licensing can help you streamline your way into retail with less risk and initial investment, utilizing a manufacturer that already has retail distribution. When you license your invention, essentially, you're leasing your invention idea to a company that is responsible for commercializing it. In most cases, when they sell your product, you earn a royalty on each piece. It means you've come up with an idea, have some intellectual property protection, developed and designed the product, at least have a working prototype that you can show and you can demonstrate. It works by finding a company that already has products similar to yours in retail, and they would be the "licensee."

You, who hold the idea and intellectual property, are the "licensor." The licensee would be responsible for the manufacturing and has either a sales team or outside sales reps, who have relationships with these retailers, and their products are on the shelves in retail. Licensing may be your shot to add your invention into their product line and a way to get your product into retailers, and for you to earn a royalty! When you license your product you earn a royalty, which is a small part of the total profit a product makes and is usually defined as a percentage of the manufacturer's wholesale price.

In some cases, it may be a different royalty rate for a direct-to-consumer distribution channel, such as an infomercial or radio ad, where there's no wholesaler but other expenses including the ad or airtime. For example, with a retailer, if the licensee sells a product wholesale for $4, the retailer may sell it for $8.99. As the licensor, you can earn between 2%-10% royalty rate from the wholesale cost. So, if you earn a 5% royalty from the $4 wholesale cost, each unit sold would be a $.20 royalty. Maybe if the licensee has a mass-market retailer, the $.20 cents per unit adds up. If a retailer like Walmart purchases for all their stores and buys 100,000 units per order, that's a $20,000 royalty payment for you.

If you find a licensee with distribution in a smaller independent store or they have smaller distribution channels, they may have higher margins to work with, but they most likely will sell less. So perhaps you could possibly negotiate a higher royalty rate. The royalty rate will depend on a wide variety of factors, including the nature of the product, typical margins of the merchandise categories, and retail distribution channels. In almost all cases, it's best to make sure you have an attorney or qualified consultant to guide you through any points of agreement and negotiate on your behalf.

As the licensor, you're responsible for the intellectual property – it's your invention. Any licensing agreement should define such areas as a term, which is the length of the agreement; geographical territory covered, which could be globally or only for North America; the, royalty rate to be paid; payment terms; and minimum guarantees or projections they may commit to selling to keep your exclusivity with them. You may also discuss receiving an advance payment possibly against future royalties to show their commitment to you. Agreements can vary and you need to be flexible to make the deal work. It should be fair for both sides and it needs to have clear expectations, just like any partnership in any way. Keep in mind that you may not have as much control over how the product is marketed, or where it's sold, and for what the wholesale price is compared to if you did it on your own. This is what these companies do for a living, and they already have relationships with buyers so they know what they are looking for.

If a licensee includes a licensed property, like a character, for example, to your intellectual property, margins may be less considering they have to pay both you and the brand property owner—both are licensors—a royalty. I invented and licensed a sphere-shaped snack container that had Sesame Street's Elmo and Cookie Monster and all the Nickelodeon's Teenage Mutant Ninja Turtles. Every time one of these sells, the licensee has to pay me and Sesame Street or Nickelodeon. But think about how many more they sell with these recognized characters and brand names on them. If there were no characters on them, they would just be generic and they would be a snack container by themselves. The licensee could pay me more for each unit and have a higher profit margin, but maybe they wouldn't sell as many if they didn't have the characters.

Again, make sure you have someone representing you who's familiar with handling the ins and outs of licensing agreements and your intellectual property.

Manufacturing Your Invention and Starting a Business

So, you've decided that you're manufacturing your invention yourself. Congratulations, you're now starting a business.

It will be your responsibility to find distribution channels and you will be responsible for sales, marketing, accounting and handling the logistics. Deciding to start your own business gives you complete control over how your product is sold, where it is sold, and it allows you to be creative with the business. However, starting and running your own business requires a commitment of money, time, effort, and energy. Maybe there's more risk, but investing in yourself and your invention, now turned into a manufactured product, may bring you greater financial rewards as an entrepreneur. So, you are thinking of manufacturing your own product.

Here are some things to consider:
- Working with a product designer or engineer, working on

making prototypes, possibly investing in molding or tooling, and identifying what material to use to make your product.

- Finding a factory, either in the United States or overseas (outsourcing).

- What is the factory's MOQ (Minimum Order Quantity) and how many units should you start with for your first order?

- Designing your product's packaging, including the barcoding and the labeling, instruction manuals, and preparing for retail.

- Obtaining product liability insurance.

- Identifying who are you are selling your product to and where you will keep your inventory once you have 3,000 units scheduled for delivery from your factory? In your living room, or in a storage facility or a warehouse, or shipped right to the retailer's distribution center?

These are just a few of the many considerations when it comes to manufacturing your own product. You have to think about how much it is going to cost to produce per unit, how much the MSRP (Manufacturer's Suggested Retail Price) will be, and what your profit will be on each unit. You will need to consider if you will sell to a wholesaler, who then sells to the consumer or sells direct to the consumer, or maybe both. Selling wholesale could be to a buyer at a retailer, like Walmart or a small boutique store, where the product was $2 to make and you sell it wholesale for $5, and they may sell it to the consumer for $9.99.

Selling direct means you could sell your product on your own website or on an infomercial or radio ad, as examples. So that means you have a profit margin from the $2 production cost to the $9.99 retail price you may sell it for. You may consider another distribution channel in-between, like an Amazon.com, a reseller, a distributor who takes a percentage of the sale, and it's like paying a salesperson or a sales rep a commission. Of course, there are other operating costs you need to consider and build into the margins to determine your net profit.

Another one of my inventions that I manufactured on my own is a collapsible egg tray. Basically, it saves space in your fridge and it opens to hold only the number of eggs you have left. I called it Eggstra Space! You can see this invention and some of my others on my website BrianFried.com/inventions. What do you think?

First I had to come up with the idea, and then I had to speak to an engineer and they made me the CAD (Computer-Aided Design) files. Then, I used the files and sent them to the factory and they made me prototypes. Then they also use those files to produce tooling, and then they made me the product. We then had to include details like the rubber on the bottom so it doesn't slip around the fridge shelves. Then I had to write up an instruction sheet, and then I put it in a plain cardboard shipper box because I was selling it through catalogs, online retailers and a home shopping channel. If it were going on the store shelves, then it would need retail packaging, a colorful printed box with graphics, which it has now. That's my Eggstra Space.

So, your ultimate goal when you're manufacturing for yourself is to make a profit from your invention, and of course, have fun doing it.

Take Your Idea Out of Your Head and Make It a Reality

Options to Create a Prototype

If you're on a shoestring budget or if you have money, the goal is to bring your idea to life – to get it in front of you and to have it look and function as close as possible to the real thing.

Let's begin by finding the least expensive method of creating your prototype: building your prototype yourself. Find existing parts or similar products that you can take apart and reassemble to create a crude prototype of your invention. Do the best you can to make it look good and focus on the functionality of how it works.

It could take some time and effort, but creating your own prototype will save you money. It could cost you maybe $50 or less, depending on what materials or parts you are trying to find and use. I had several inventions I was working on, and I remember buying all these toys and taking them apart into pieces. I would rip up teddy bears to take recording chips out of them. I even got caught by my daughter when she was younger taking apart some of her stuff. She was not happy with me, but you get the idea. Look around and see what you have already in your possession, or go shopping and see what you can find and what you need to make a prototype out of what already exists. Try to get as close to a works-like, looks-like prototype of your invention.

Should you have the funds to spend or if you can save up some money for a more professional-looking and working-like prototype, you can consider hiring a product designer or engineer to create CAD (Computer-Aided Design) drawings for you. Your idea's design and parts are saved into special files that can be used to create your prototype. You can also use them for manufacturing and getting quotes for future production. The CAD drawings can include 2-dimensional or flat drawings as well as 3D drawings and videos of your prototype. Engineers can help figure out the best way your invention should function with twists and turns, and maybe they can help identify what materials and parts your prototype may need. Both engineers and product designers can help to design your product the way you envisioned it to look. Both may be able to make the prototype for you in their office or workshop, or you can take the CAD files and you can go make a prototype anywhere you want.

There are many websites now where you can just upload these CAD files. A trustworthy and reputable one that I like to use is Shapeways.com. You place your order on their website and you can pick the material and the color you want, and your prototype shows up in your mailbox within a few weeks.

You can even go to your local library that may have 3D printers you can rent time to use, for a small fee. You can also call your local college's engineering department and you can ask them for a student to help you create your prototype. Another resource, which is interesting, is that you can find 3D print shops locally by searching online for maker spaces - creative workshops - nearby. You can go there ,and work on your prototype yourself by paying for the machine time, and sometimes they have people there that you can pay to do it for you. They most likely have CNC laser cutting machines, 3D printers, and even a woodshop and other machines and processes to help build out your prototype for you or with you. You can even buy a 3D printer for yourself these days. I like MakerBot and Ultimaker brand 3D printers but there are plenty of 3D printers to buy on the market now. They can be the size of an inkjet printer that costs from a few hundred dollars and up. Besides learning and working the software, you have the printer maintenance and you need to use a special filament to feed the printer, which then gets melted and builds these plastic layers on top of each other to make your 3D prototype.

The ultimate goal is to get as close as possible to the real thing for yourself to be proud of, and for others to provide you with feedback. Remember, there might be a few iterations that you have to go through to get your prototype just right, but it doesn't have to be perfect until you move to producing your finished product. Your prototype can even be used to demonstrate to a licensee for a potential licensing deal, or it can be used to prepare you for your future production to sell into retail.

Your idea, now brought to life with your prototype.

Protecting Your Idea: What's a Patent? Why do I Need One?

There are many opinions on whether a patent is worth it or not, or if you should get a patent at all. I personally think that if you have a chance to get a patent, it can add value to your assets and protect your intellectual property. A patent can make a stronger case for you, should you decide to sell your invention yourself or if you are looking to license your intellectual property (IP) to earn royalties. Sometimes your invention may not even be patentable, but as long as you're not infringing on their IP or their patent, you can keep moving forward.

There are three types of patents: utility, design, or plant patents. I'm going to focus on the utility and design patents, but let's start with a quick definition of what a patent is.

A patent is an intellectual property right granted by the Government of the United States of America to an inventor «to exclude others from making, using, offering for sale or selling the invention throughout the United States, or importing the invention into the

United States» for a limited time in exchange for public disclosure of the invention when the patent is granted.

Now that you have your prototype, you'll begin showing your invention to different people you know personally or who you are going to start working with, including potential partners, licensees, or factories. In the next section, I'll outline the steps you should take to consider protecting your intellectual property.

Tips When Disclosing Your Idea to Others

Before you begin showing your invention to the world, you should have at least the most basic protection, to be patent pending. To say that your invention has patent-pending status, you can file a provisional patent application. That gives you the right for one year to say your idea is patent pending while you explore the opportunity of licensing or manufacturing, or if you're going to move forward at all, from the feedback you received during the first year.

One thing I challenge inventors with when they reach out to me is that I ask them if they have any intellectual property protection. And they tell me yes, they have a patent or they filed for a patent and I ask what type of patent and they say either they don't know or they have a provisional.

Once I explain to them the different types of patents and applications, and that the provisional patent is just a placeholder, it's clearer to them what they actually have. Also, it's important to know what you or somebody else is going to file or has filed for you regarding your intellectual property. Did you have a provisional patent application filed for you, or a non-provisional patent, which has the claims included when filed? Or do you have a design patent issued, meaning you received your patent? Or is it only filed when was it submitted to the U.S. Patent & Trademark Office, the USPTO? What they filed or didn't file for you is important for you to know.

When you file a provisional patent application, the examiners at the U.S. Patent & Trademark Office don't look at the content of what you or your patent attorney or agent has filed for you. When your application is submitted online, mailed or faxed, you'll receive a confirmation of the filing date. Remember, a provisional patent application is just a placeholder for the one- year term. The information described about your invention that is included in the provisional patent application is usually broad and doesn't include the specifics of claims. So, while you're out getting your feedback from testing your prototype, you can think about adding or modifying your design or the claims to include in the non-provisional patent application, that utility patent. If there is too much of a difference from the original, then you may have to refile another provisional patent application, or you can skip directly to the non-provisional patent that includes the claims, but you would not be able to include your original filing date. You may need to discuss your specific questions with a patent attorney or agent before making decisions that can affect your patent application.

Before the provisional patent application year term comes due, you need to decide if you're going to file a non-provisional patent application, also called the utility patent. A utility patent includes claims and is like the metes and bounds of property, or like the territory you own and what your intellectual property is all about. If you miss the one-year date to convert your provisional patent to a utility patent, then technically your invention becomes public and you won't be able to protect your invention any further. By the way, the non- provisional patent application can be filed directly without filing that provisional patent application, or again you can use that one-year provisional placeholder and continue within that year to convert it.

Once you file the non-provisional patent application, you'll eventually be assigned to a specific office and examiner in the U.S. Patent & Trademark Office, depending on the industry and classification of your invention. From my experience, it takes about 12 to 18 months until they even look at your application. Most of the time your first notice from them will be an office action that some or all of your claims are rejected.

Don't be alarmed. Most of the time they need clarification or you have to challenge them and give reasons why your claims are unique, novel, and non-obvious. This is why I seek a professional, a patent attorney or agent to handle my intellectual property filings and communicate to the patent office on my behalf.

If your invention is ornamental and really focused on just the design, or maybe you are not able to get a utility patent if it was rejected, or you know that you should just focus on the design, then you can apply for a design patent. While your application is in process, you can also say your invention is patent pending. A design patent usually takes around 18 months to be issued and is much easier to obtain, in my opinion, than a utility patent with the claims. Utility patents are looked at as having more value than design patents. Realistically, someone can change the design of your invention enough that they can get a design patent around yours. Remember, I'm not a patent attorney or agent. I'm just talking to you from an inventor's perspective.

The cost of hiring a patent attorney or agent can really vary. You can call an attorney that charges $500 for something and the same service can cost $4,000 from someone else, but here's a ballpark of what I usually pay. Before we go there, you're probably wondering what the difference is between a patent attorney and a patent agent? It's a good question and good to know. A patent attorney graduated from law school and can actually litigate, meaning that they can represent you in the court of law. Maybe someone is infringing on your intellectual property or it's you infringing and you need legal advice or you have to be in court. A patent agent is someone that has registered with the U.S. Patent & Trademark Office to file and communicate on your behalf and they follow their guidelines. I find that many engineers I meet actually register as patent agents. Typically, a patent attorney charges more since they went to law school. Depending on your budget, you can decide what works best for you. A provisional patent application can cost about $700 and up to prepare, plus the filing fee from the USPTO which can be as low as $75.

You can speak to a patent attorney that can charge several thousand dollars for preparing the application because they may have prepared your provisional patent application like a non- provisional with all the claims in it or maybe not. But, remember I mentioned to you it's good to keep that Provisional Patent Application (PPA) broad, while you test the market and it's also going to cost you less of an investment to start.

A design patent can cost around $2,000 to prepare plus the filing fees (use the link above to look up the USPTO fees) depending on how many drawings are needed that illustrate your design. A non-provisional patent application usually costs from $2,000 to $4,000 or more to prepare, plus the fees.

When discussing your invention with a patent attorney they are bound by their legal title representing the law, and technically you don't need them to sign a Non-Disclosure Agreement (NDA) since everything you discuss with them is completely confidential. An NDA is not necessary with a registered patent agent either, as they are bound by patent office rules to work with you only to file your patent application. The thing to pay attention to is how many claims will be included in your application, so ask and get more information with your quote. Make smart business decisions, and before you do, get multiple quotes. Look at what they charge, what they are proposing to include for you, and decide if they are someone, you'd like to work with. Do they call you back when they say they will? Are they respectful to you? Or are they too busy for you from the start? Get references from them. Get a recommendation from someone you know that had a good experience with them. How many patents do they have issued under their name with inventors as a patent attorney or agent? Just because you told them about your invention, doesn't mean you're obligated to work with them.

Here is another option. You can write up and submit the provisional patent application or any of the other patent applications yourself, but I don't recommend it. It's just my opinion. The U.S. Patent & Trademark Office (USPTO) has great reference guides right on their website on how you can do it yourself including how the draft drawings, the claims, the format, and the summary should be prepared. If I need something done, I go to a specialist. We can always learn something new, but I need someone that does a good job for me, especially if I'm going to start a business from my invention and I want to make sure that I do it right. Especially if I want to license my idea, intellectual property is one of the most important parts, most of the time. That's what they are licensing from you, your intellectual property. That's why I use a patent attorney or agent because they are the specialists and they're able to communicate to the USPTO on my behalf.

Finally, there are the USPTO filing fees which you can find on the uspto.gov website. They offer deep discounts for first- timers, senior citizens, and those with low socioeconomic status. And once you have your patent, congrats! You'll also have maintenance fees that you'll pay at certain time periods to keep your patent active during the 20-year term for the utility patent and no maintenance fees for the design patent. This is what a Patent looks like.

For filing fees see the link from the USPTO website: https://www.uspto.gov/learning-and-resources/fees-and-payment.

To read up on micro or small entity qualifications, you can read more here:

https://www.uspto.gov/patents/apply/applying-online/ entity-status-fee-purposes.

It feels good to be a patent holder and it's better when you make money with your invention and you can too!

Can You Protect Your Invention, and What are Your Options?

A professional patent search with a patentability opinion, as well as your own research checking online and out in the market, will help you determine your next steps. Before we make the decision to move forward, let's look at your options based on whether or not you can obtain intellectual property protection from a patent. So, you might have hit a brick wall because they found an almost identical patent compared to your idea when you received your patent search back. Or you realize there's a limited shot or no shot at all of obtaining a patent. So, what options do you have?

Let's say, for example, someone comes to me with an idea and I look at it and I say there are a lot of similar things out there that we are easily pulling up online, but they think that their idea is still different. I suggest that they do a patent search, I think that's the right thing to do. They say, but what happens if I find out that my idea isn't patentable? Are they done? Do they stop? Here's the thing: when I get a patent ability opinion and it comes back and it says I can't get a patent, I'm ok with it, at least I know where I stand and I have some decisions to make. I can manufacture it myself, or

I can just move onto my next idea. I'll come up with another one. If I wanted to license my invention to earn royalties and it's likely I won't get a patent because it's too similar or it's exactly the same, or the patent that was similar expired, then what does the manufacturer need me for? They can make the product themselves and they don't have to pay me. So, what are your alternatives? You can make the hard decision to give up now or consider these options to keep moving forward. Look at the expiration date of the patent that's challenging your idea. How long until it expires? Can you wait? Did it expire already? Remember, utility patents are 20- year terms and design patents are 15 years. When you look at the patent numbers, if there is a letter D in front of the numbers, then it's a design patent.

Consider manufacturing your product yourself if it's an expired patent and you still want to move forward. Many inventors don't think they have the money to manufacture, or they're not familiar with manufacturing, or they don't know what steps to take or how much it's going to cost them to manufacture. The good news is you're reading this book, so the steps to manufacture are outlined for you.

Once you speak with a factory and you get an idea of how much it would cost to manufacture your product, you may realize you don't have the money available, or maybe you do, or it was less than you expected, and it's possible and in your budget. If you don't have the money, then you can figure it out. Save up, so what if it takes you a month or a year! Ask your friends and family for a loan or try to get a different loan. Or consider crowdfunding if you think you could have a good business from this product. Maybe you can continue working on your idea without a patent and come up with a good trademarkable name. Again, you can continue working on your idea as long as you're not infringing on someone else's patent or you risk getting issued a cease-and-desist notice and taking a chance on getting sued.

Let me give you an example of a good success story. You've heard of the Snuggie, right? Well, that design of a blanket with sleeves has been around for a long time and a marketing company realized that the idea was older than 20 years and the patent was expired and in the public domain. So they manufactured a blanket with sleeves and trademarked the name – Snuggie. And then came Slanket and many other companies that produced a blanket with sleeves that could do the same thing with a different name. Many people have heard of the name Snuggie, and they built an asset with that trademark.

Here's a quick definition of a trademark: A trademark is a word, phrase, symbol, and/or design that identifies and distinguishes the source of the goods of one party from those of others, and rights come from actual use. A trademark can last forever, so long as you file the specific documents and you pay the fees at regular intervals.

Do you know how you see the ™ next to a name of a product or company? When it's being used in commerce in a particular class of goods, they can put that ™ next to the name of their brand or their product with or without filing with the U.S. Patent & Trademark Office (USPTO). If they want to make it official, you can see how some products have an "R" in the circle, ® that's a registered trademark. That's the difference between the ™ and ®. It gives notice to others you're using that name in a certain class of goods.

Here's another option if you hit that brick wall and your search was someone else's intellectual property and their patent is still active. You can always reach out to the patent holder and try to partner up. Or you have an improvement on their invention and you need their patent to add it. Or maybe you want to manufacture it for them, or with them, and you license it from them and pay them a royalty!

Sometimes people take a chance, and they file the provisional patent application if they're not sure if their idea is patentable and they still have a chance to explore the market and either stop or start selling it. Again, there are risks to these types of decisions, especially if that other product's owner finds out and puts a lawsuit against you and shuts your business down, and potentially sues you for all the profits that you made.

Not being able to get a patent doesn't mean that you need to give up. These are the decisions you need to make when you come up with an idea and navigate through the checkpoints of bringing your idea to market or moving on to your next idea.

Or, great news, if you received your patentability opinion back, and the patent attorney, agent or search firm says your idea has potential for a patent, consider getting a second opinion. Or you can, keep moving forward with the next steps of either making a prototype, filing the provisional patent application so you are patent-pending and you can start to think about licensing or manufacturing your invention with the possibility of having intellectual property protection of a patent or a trademark, right?

The goal is to figure out a way to make you money with your invention and be sure you are working on an idea that will. We have decisions to make along the way. Ultimately, it's up to you to decide what your next steps should be.

Presenting Your Invention

Get Ready to Pitch Your Invention, and to Whom

It's time to start talking about your invention or product to buyers representing retailers, licensees (manufacturers with the distribution that you would earn royalties from), or licensing agents that might represent your products and pitch your idea for you on your behalf to licensees. The first step in creating your pitch is to figure out who you'll be pitching to. You need to be prepared and do your research to make sure you're not pitching a shovel to a kitchen gadget company. Have your best prototype if you're looking to license your invention or have your finished product if you're manufacturing and ready to start receiving purchase orders.

Pitches can happen in an in-person meeting, or through video conference, or over the phone while you share information like video links and pictures or images with them via email. It could be with one person from the company or a team of decision-makers. Now let's get ready to tell the world what you've invented!

Pitching to Direct Response Infomercial Marketers to Earn Royalties

Direct Response (DR) or TV Infomercial (DRTV) companies are mostly searching for mass audience appeal or popular categories and will pick up where you left off in your invention process, looking to license your invention from you. I still would do my due diligence and have a proper patent search done and have some level of protection. The PPA (Provisional Patent Application) filed puts them on notice that your product is patent-pending, or you can have them sign an NDA, the non-disclosure agreement.

Pay attention to TV infomercials you see, get a sense of how they deliver their pitch and what type of audience they're focused on. Notice that most follow the pattern of problem- solution ideas. Ask yourself if you think your invention could be demonstrated in a way that the TV commercial delivers the message. Before presenting to a DRTV company, do your research by visiting their websites, going to retailers that sell "As Seen on TV" products, and jotting down the companies listed on the packaging to review their website online. Make sure you're calling or reaching out to these companies directly.

Pitching to Potential Licensees to Earn Royalties

If you want to license your invention that's an industry-specific product, like a housewares or hardware company, look for the leading brands selling online and in retail brick and mortar stores where you could envision your invention together with their products. Go on that company's website, find the number and call their office, and find out what their process is to pitch or submit your invention. Also, take a look and notice if they list the retailers that they're in, so you can calculate if they can do some good volume if your invention was included in their product line. And while you're looking through their products, make sure your invention idea would fit in with theirs. If and when you get someone on the phone or get their email address, be prepared to share video links, pictures, and benefits of why your product is for them.

There are licensing agents within industries that can walk your idea directly to these licensees and earn a small percentage of your royalty negotiated. Or you may want to attend upcoming industry tradeshows where most of these industry manufacturers, these potential licensees, showcase their new products to their buyers. You can go onto a tradeshow listing website, like TSNN.com Trade Show News Network that lets you search by industry, area, and region to see what shows are coming up.

Once you find tradeshows that are related to your industry, go directly to their websites and see what credentials you may need, and try to attend, especially if there's one that's close to you. Many are inventor-friendly and even have a dedicated area to showcase new inventions. When you're at the tradeshow, you have the opportunity to see new products from the industry, find potential licensees to pitch or you may even bump into a few buyers along the way - and maybe your invention will be exhibited at the next one!

Launch Your Product on Home Shopping Channels

Home shopping channels like QVC and HSN are also good launching pads for your invention, and here you'll need to be manufacturing your product on your own. Uniqueness needs to be there. They like innovation, invention, especially a brand-new product being sold for the first time on their network, and so does their audience. Their customers watch demonstrations of your invention on TV or live streaming online, or they check out what's for sale on their website and customers place their orders online or call in. You partner with the shopping channel. They put you and your product into their production schedule, live or recorded, and you send them inventory, usually a $30,000-$70,000 wholesale test to start. If it sells, they continue ordering from you and if it doesn't, they send you back your inventory, no hard feelings. If you sell your product at a wholesale cost of $10 and they sell it for $20, you will get paid $10 for each of the units sold. I've had several products on QVC that did well, and it changed my life. I happened to meet a buyer at a tradeshow and she invited me to her office to pitch my inventions.

For home shopping channels, your product should be ready for sale, although I did work with a buyer that wrote a Purchase Order (PO) based on my pre-production sample. Remember, anything is possible! You can go to their website and sift through the process or call somebody that already has contacts there and can make the process easier and quicker to get through the doors. Products with inventory or ready for production, direct and simple easy to understand demonstrations and pricing should be prepared and ready to go when you present to the category buyers. You can be the presenter on air yourself and demo with the host or you can hire someone to do it for you. I've done both. It was a great experience and an inventor- friendly one for me and could be an option for you as well to consider with your distribution strategy for your invention.

Be Prepared to Pitch

Whatever distribution channel you decide to pitch, be prepared when presenting your invention. Know your product in and out, understand your industry, know your competition, and who you're presenting to so you have a better shot of success. Keep your emotions out of your decisions and put yourself in the marketer's or retailer's position. Think about what's in it for them first, who their audience is and what their customers want, and then make your decision to move forward and close the deal, so you can see your invention out in the market.

Pitching to Catalogs: How Do They Work?

Some are still sending out printed catalogs or have an online e-commerce website and are looking for unique, specialty products, new inventions to insert into their product offering to their customers. Most of the time these catalogs cater to a specific niche, like someone who is into auto parts, or knitting and they sell interesting items to have their customers keep coming back. Some brands may have their own product catalog that may be possible for licensing, but when selling wholesale to catalogs, you need to be ready with inventory and be prepared to send samples to the catalog buyers that are interested. Some of these catalogs, either online or in print, can do some good volume with their customer followers. And some are smaller and may only do very little volume. I'm just setting expectations here, but this can be the case with any distribution channel.

Do your research and see what catalogs you can identify that have good potential and see what their sales volume looks like. Once accepted, they'll send you a vendor agreement to be filled out to get set up with them, followed by a purchase order with quantities requested and a window of where and when to ship. Catalogs can be a great launching pad for your new product and usually have higher margins to get you started. Envision the catalogs where you can see your invention. What catalogs do you get in the mail now? Or what catalogs do you visit online now? What are your hobbies, inventions?

Pitching To Retail Buyers

Retail buyers expect to see your finished product and purchase from you at wholesale cost. Identify the retailers where you can see your product being sold. Are they a specialty store, an independent store for a niche market? Or are they a mass-market general retailer? What type of volume do they do? So, let's get ready to pitch to the buyers.

When you are thinking about your buyer, go one step past them and think about their customer that they have to win over. What does the customer want to see and will they buy your product, and is the price right? It will make for a much better conversation with the buyer. You may have to travel to their office to meet them, or some can make decisions over the phone or on a video conference call. Or maybe you can set up a meeting at an upcoming tradeshow they'll be attending. Be prepared to discuss various packaging options, shipping times, wholesale costs, price breaks for larger quantity discounts, and have your best pitch ready describing the benefits of your product. Check their website for new vendor account information and call headquarters to connect with the right category buyer for your invention. Think about your product on the shelf. It's amazing to think about somebody else buying your product for the reason you came up with it. Be ready.

Understanding Licensing, How to Find and Pitch to Licensees

When I'm at the stores or searching online for a licensee, I envision the stores where I can see my product. Is it a mass- market retail store that does high-volume sales? Or a high- end specialty store that may do less volume? Or is it a store for a particular niche that's the right market for the invention? Whichever stores you're browsing in, I would look for the brands, the manufacturers that have products with product lines already on the shelves or hanging in the isles, or the impulse items by the register, or anywhere in the physical stores or the online stores that I can see my product aligning with their product line.

Retailers don't license products from you. They have vendors which are the brands or manufacturers that stock their shelves or sell on their websites, then sell their products to you and consumers.

So let's search for and focus on the brands and product lines that are in the stores. Just a quick definition to share here: A *licensee* is a manufacturer with distribution that I would be presenting to and they would rent the rights to my intellectual property for an agreed term, including what territory they sell into and exclusivity in an industry or other components within a licensing agreement, and I am the *licensor*, with the intellectual property.

Somewhere on the package of the similar product category or

product line you think could be a good potential licensee is the company information listed that's manufacturing the product. Those are the companies I jot down; I take a quick snapshot of the product and the packaging on my phone, I look at the other products they're selling in that area and check if their brand is anywhere else in the store, or other categories online. I save the web links where they are distributing their products online. Sometimes you'll see "distributed by" on the packages. That's usually a distribution company, a sales team that the manufacturer hired, and pays a commission on their sales. They have relationships with the retailers and distribution channels they manage. They're sometimes called a manufacturer's rep. If you're trying to license, I would call the manufacturer, not necessarily that distribution company since the manufacturer is the one who would license an invention.

I compile what I found from my online search and in the stores, then I start doing some research on those companies. I pay attention to what other stores or types of retail distribution carry their products. I also look at their website and browse around their products to make sure that it makes sense for me to pitch my product to them. I check their site to see if they are inventor-friendly and if they're looking for new product submissions. Please know that I am talking about direct company websites that have products in the retail as potential licensees, not third party marketing companies.

The companies you identified that could be good licensee candidates probably attend and exhibit in industry tradeshows and may list the upcoming tradeshows on their website. For tradeshows, TSNN.com, Tradeshow News Network, is a resource I've used for many years until I had a better understanding of which industry shows the manufacturers attend.

I take my list of potential licensees and go on LinkedIn. I connect with some executives of the company, I find their product development Vice President, but mostly I go for the President first. Usually, when you call for the President, their receptionist may put you through to the President but most likely will direct you to the right person to speak to. Before I make phone calls, or send emails or have a video conference call, I make a quick video of my prototype, or I'm prepared to show a 3D animated video, or I take clear pictures, and I prepare some really simple bullet points for people to be able to understand my invention, either for me to share, or to speak about.

Now that you're up to this part of the book, you're prepared to speak to someone about your invention. You can assure the company that you've done your due diligence, including a patent search, you have a patentability opinion, you have a prototype, you have pictures and/or, videos, you have a description of your invention, and you at least have patent-pending status. When you make the calls and you get someone on the line or have a meeting, be real and get right to the point. Remember, you're pitching to people in the industry. So, stick to talking about your product and its potential, rather than statistics in the industry they most likely know better than you. Before your meeting, remind yourself to take your emotions out of the conversation. It's about your product and whether or not it will make money for the company you're pitching. Make sure you are pitching to the right company. If you're pitching a toy to a housewares company, most likely it's not a match. Make sure your invention complements their product line. Don't waste each other's time.

You may find after your meeting that you've received some interest in your invention. Congratulations! You may have a potential licensing deal on the table. This is very exciting!

Potential licensees may say that they're just not interested. I am not one to make up excuses, but let me share some that I've heard when they say no to you so you're prepared and keep smiling after your call either way. When they say that they're not interested, that doesn't mean your invention stinks. They may not like it, or it just might not be for them, or they don't work with inventors or license outside products, or they have their own in-house product development team. It could be timing or they're not looking for new products right now or they have a full product pipeline that they are already working on, or they're not investing in any more tooling this year or they're just focused on something else in particular right now. You don't have to take it personally, it's just not for them at that very moment.

I've shown the same product to the same company and they said no to me, and I showed it again, two years later, they said yes and I licensed the invention to them. In another personal experience, I had the intellectual property of trademarks that I built a brand with the emoticons and acronyms that mostly the kids were using back in the day. Now everybody uses them, like LOL (laugh out loud), TTYL (talk to you later), and SUP (what's up?). But mine had a little twist to them like the LOL had a smiley face in the middle, and SUP had a question mark after it. I trademarked them outside of cell phones and computers in other classes of goods and tried to find a T-shirt manufacturer licensee for a long time to license my trademarks and my vision.

I got lots of no's, probably close to 75 or more, until I found someone, a major brand at the time, that was willing to take a chance on me, and licensed my intellectual property. So, my trademarks ended up on T-shirts and sold in retailers, like Target and other stores in the U.S. and Canada. That was an amazing experience and journey that had many twists and turns. Ultimately, you just have to keep your head up and keep going. Same thing with many product inventions I've licensed or represented. You just have to find the right partner, licensee.

Remember, as great as you are, your invention is what they have to make a decision on if it's right for their company and has the potential to make money. Now find the right partner for you and your invention.

What Does it Take to Manufacture Your Product?

A few quick questions to think about. Do you have the money to manufacture your product or do you have to raise the money? Are you going to ask a family member for a loan to fund your venture, or are you going to tap into your personal savings account? Are you going to start a crowd- funding campaign? Or mortgage your house?

Before you speak to someone or decide on how you are going to raise money, it's good to have some answers for the questions you're going to be asked or maybe ask yourself. How much does your idea cost to make? Now that you are turning your idea into a product, there may be costs associated with tooling, production, packaging and design, warehousing, product liability insurance, websites, marketing, legal and accounting, and all of the other costs associated with running a business. So, let's get started!

When I decide to manufacture my product, I look for a contract manufacturer or a manufacturer that makes similar type products relative to my invention. These contract manufacturers just make products, they don't sell anything most of the time. They're like order takers that work with your supplied CAD files or your product specifications, then they calculate how much material, labor, and machine time is needed to determine how much it's going to cost to produce your product. Contract manufacturers can also help with packaging options and figuring out shipping. If you're connecting with manufacturers that only make metal parts for airplanes and you need a metal part made that is not for an airplane, they may help you but probably not, since that's not their business. So, finding these contract manufacturers just focuses on orders to fulfill. If I'm going to go to a factory that makes other things, I would consider asking one that's already making similar products like furniture. I'm in the middle of a furniture project right now. I wish I could show you, but we'd need to sign an NDA first! So, I found a factory that makes chairs and they were open to helping me and I told them that if they did, I would place an order with them so they have some incentive to help me out. You just have to be patient with them since this is not their business. This is like speculative side work for them - away from the daily manufacturing that keeps them in business.

Some products may require an initial investment in tooling, which I can describe as two big metal plates that are shaped like your product on the inside and to your product specifications. If it's a plastic material product you're producing, it starts off where the melted plastic is poured between metal plates to form your product. You may hear the term *cavity*, which means every time the tooling opens and closes a finished piece comes out. Sometimes you can have larger tooling made to accommodate a larger cavity size producing more product in one pass. It will cost more upfront for larger tooling but take less labor and machine time. You can discuss the balance of the tooling size and costs with the factory based on your budget. Your product may need parts assembled and that will also increase the cost of the product as well. There could be a wide range of costs for tooling you receive, since it can be made with various materials. For example, it could be made from aluminum, or it could be made from steel, which can also affect the lifespan and how many units this tooling can produce before you have to make new tooling. If you're talking about another round of tooling production, that means you most likely are selling your product and it's selling well!

You may hear the word *molding*, which is a shape formed out of a material that can hold the hot material in place before it takes shape, like silicone. Molding would be less than tooling and the factory will help determine what the best solution is for you since this is not what we do for a living. You want to find a factory that is really looking to help you. If you want to know more about the details of tooling and manufacturing for a specific product or process, a simple YouTube search will bring up videos that show how different products are made. I've learned about many different types of manufacturing working on all these projects and I've watched plenty of videos. For example, it's easy to just put in how a ballpoint pen is assembled in an online search, click on videos and you can watch a factory in action.

Finding A Manufacturer Locally or Overseas to Manufacture Your Product

Not all products need tooling. Maybe your product needs a seamstress, a machine shop, die-cutting, or steel welding. So, where do you find the companies to do this? I look for local contract manufacturers on Thomasnet.com and I also look for overseas manufacturers on a site like Alibaba.com. I ask other people that I network with who they use, like those at your local inventor's club. Over the years, I've built relationships with different types of manufacturing in upstate New York, Colorado, China, Taiwan, and Vietnam and I feel like I can produce almost anything now!

When you're searching for a factory, notice that there are trading companies, suppliers, and manufacturers that you'll see listed. I like to work with the factories directly to get their pricing and not have to deal with brokers that markup the cost from the factory. A tip I've been doing for years: ask the factory if they can take you on a tour of their factory on a video call. I've even watched my products on video being produced overseas. I check to see if that person I'm speaking to is actually working in a factory or if they're just a broker. I test them. I see if they're a busy factory and, what types of people they have working there. I look at the cleanliness of the shop and if we can communicate well and they can understand me.

I also ask them to send me a sample of something they produced and experience a transaction, like how am I going to pay them, if they ship on time, and if they do what they say they are going to do. When the package arrives, I check how they packaged the item and I look at the quality. I also like to ask for references from other customers they've worked with. Sometimes they offer them to me and sometimes they don't because of customer confidentiality. You can also find a local factory to manufacture with and you can physically do all of the above in person in the US. You have to find a balance between the costs of manufacturing locally vs. overseas, and the processes and comfort level are most important. You just want to make sure that you'll have a good potential manufacturing partner for you and your product.

As you begin reaching out to manufacturers, be sure to get a quote from local manufacturers and from overseas manufacturers. Sometimes I would get quotes from local manufacturers for more than what I would ask someone to pay for my product, so I compare overseas pricing which may be less and I can actually produce a product and have business from it. It's important to know what the customer would be willing to pay and work backward from there. So, if it's a $29.99 product, it should be available to a wholesaler for around $15 and it should cost you about $7.50 all in with manufacturing shipping and expenses, so you can put $7.50 in and get at least $7.50 out. There are some inventors I connect with later in the manufacturing process and they tell me that they put in $7.50

and they're selling it for $8.50. $7.50 in to make $1 profit? I am exaggerating here a little bit but actually, I'm serious. Do you think that's a good business decision? Be smart and understand your margins to stay in business.

When speaking with manufacturers, you're most likely going to be working with their MOQ (Minimum Order Quantity), especially for your first few orders. If you're not able to fill one of those shipping containers (think of the big storage units that are on the back of trucks or trains), then you'll probably want to find a factory that's willing to work with a low quantity to start. This allows you to validate if there's a market for your product and to get your feet wet selling it. Just be ready and know that when you're manufacturing in low volume, you're probably going to be paying more per unit. Whereas if you're doing mass production, the costs will be less for production. You want everything to be just right. So, before you begin production, request pre-production samples for you to approve.

Don't forget to factor in potential packaging. Is your product going in a clamshell or blister card? Or just bulk packaging in a polybag? Ask the manufacturer if that's something they can help with in-house or outsourcing for you and can show you some options, or you can find packaging design companies or freelancers online. They can work within the dimensions and die lines you give them. Ultimately the features, graphics, and instructions are all your responsibility. It's your product. Other costs that need to be factored into the quote include shipping and warehousing, for both local and overseas manufacturers. Are you using a fulfillment center? Or how about those monthly rental storage units? Or, will you use your garage or your living room in your house to fulfill orders? You can send the shipment directly to a retailer's distribution center if you have orders already. And shipping...how much is it going to cost to ship from the factory? From your overseas manufacturer? Are you shipping to the U.S. by an air carrier, like FedEx? Or UPS or DHL? Or by sea, on a cargo ship? And you'll need to include import taxes and duty costs and hire a shipping agent for the paperwork. If you've manufactured locally, it might be easier and cost less to ship from the manufacturer wherever you need to ship in the U.S.

Using all of the information you've gathered along with the quote, determine the total cost of having your product manufactured. While cost is a major factor in choosing the factory, you have to choose what's best for you. So, you have to form a good business relationship with them knowing that that's the company and the factory you're going to work with.

Remember, you're the boss and you're the one making a business decision and not the emotional one. I know you've heard that a couple of times, but it's a reminder to help you make better decisions from a business perspective. Just because you talked about your idea with someone doesn't mean you are obligated to them. Turning the idea that you had into a product for sale can be a greater risk financially and of your time, and it can produce greater rewards too. There's a reason you're doing all this. Let's get that pre-production sample and continue to the next steps.

Crowdfunding to Raise Money for Manufacturing

You might want to use crowdfunding websites not only to raise money for your manufacturing costs, but also as a way to get the word out or to get your first round of orders, or for staffing, product development, marketing, or even operational expenses. You can consider this type of crowdfunding option to obtain financing that could work for you and your invention. There's donation-based, rewards-based, or equity-based crowdfunding. Donation-based crowdfunding is a finance option where people give you money with no expectation of a financial return. With rewards-based crowdfunding, investors contribute funds in anticipation of receiving the product or service your company is offering and there's also no expectation of a financial return. With equity-based crowdfunding, investors become shareholders in your company. They receive financial returns and get a share of future profits.

Have a solid video explanation of your product and a chance for your potential crowd funders to learn more about you and your plan. Prepare your bullet points and offers available to get involved with you. Just be prepared to do quite a bit of asking for contributions from your network and especially social media, a lot of asking. If it works out and you reach your campaign goal, that's great! However, if it fails and you try to present it to a licensee, they may easily look it up online that there was a campaign on your invention and it bombed, so if nobody else wanted it, they'll see that. Think of the way that you make first impressions and think one or two steps ahead. Again, it's all about risk vs. reward. You can check out Indiegogo.com and Kickstarter.com, they're both rewards-based crowdfunding campaigns most popular with inventors with inventions.

Selling to Retailers with One Product

Something else to consider when pitching a buyer is that when you have one product or one SKU (Stock Keeping Unit), it can be very difficult for a buyer to commit to a purchase order. The SKU is a unique number used to internally track inventory.

The buyers most likely would prefer working with a vendor who has a line with multiple products and has an established track record or history of successful sales. This is how it is most of the time and it may be tough for an inventor with one product to break into a retailer. The buyers do take chances with a new product if they like it, but with one, there may be a slim shot.

They would have to open up a new vendor account with you, teach you their logistics, and you would have to deliver to their warehouse within a tight window of time. All this has to be perfect to meet their requirements and work with their systems. The buyers are assigned a certain space of shelving within a retail store and they have sales targets of how much they need to produce from that space. So, they have a responsibility to find the right products and add them to the shelves. Their careers depend on it. So that's why they go for established brands with a track record. Not that getting one product into retail is impossible, but it can be difficult. That's why we have other options these days. We have Amazon for example, where we can put our one product for sale or we can sell our product on our own website, or we can find other Amazon-type websites to sell through, and we can even sell directly through social media advertising.

We are inventors, finding solutions to challenges. Anything is possible, and you can figure out your way into retail. Keep going.

Time to Make Money with Your Inventions

Understanding Licensees & Licensors, Calculating Royalties and Licensing Agreements

I gave you an example of what product licensing is earlier. Here it is again for your reference and we'll also discuss what a deal may look like. Product licensing can be simply explained as the licensee, which is a manufacturer, is also responsible for the distribution. They may have their own factory locally or overseas and have a built-in sales team or hire sales reps to present products - hopefully, your invention - to buyers, retailers, and e-tailers.

You, as the licensor, are responsible for the intellectual property you bring to the table for the licensee to rent the rights for a particular industry. When they sell your product, you earn a royalty. And royalty is a percentage of the wholesale price the manufacturer sells the product for. If the licensee also sells, let's say, direct-to-consumer and not to a wholesaler, there is more margin to go around so you may receive a higher royalty rate on those types of sales. So, let›s start off by going over the sales cycle and what it means for you. If the product costs $2 to manufacture and sells for $4 wholesale, then the retailer sells it for $8.99.

As the licensor, you may receive between 2% and 10% royalty rate of the wholesale cost, relative to the industry and profit margins. Let's say we agreed to a 5% royalty rate on the wholesale cost which is $4, which calculates to $.20 cents per unit as your royalty payment.

Before you consider approaching that licensee, research the volume of sales that they currently do with their existing products and what distribution channels they sell into. They may have major big-box retailers and your product sells well, and every $.20 royalty can add up to bigger royalty checks. If they sell to smaller independent stores or niche retailers, it may still sell well, but the point here is to understand and discuss expectations with your potential partner, licensee.

You want to do a deal where you and the licensee both earn and it makes sense for both of you and for them. For us inventors, it may seem like a 5% royalty rate is a small percentage, but you can also end up having a 100% royalty rate and they sell zero. So, you have to think about what the licensee does and their expenses they have to manage, like having to pay their company employees and, other overhead including the production of your product. They work with the buyers, closing the deal to receive purchase orders and handling all of the logistics. On top of all that, they have tight margins to work with from the retailers, and of course, pay you, and still make a profit. They have most of the risk. Yes, you do too with all that you've done. A lot of pieces of the margins to go around for everybody to earn from.

Also, many licensees may agree to move forward with a licensing deal verbally. However, before they send you the paperwork or sign, you may hear them say that they have a meeting coming up with their buyer and they're going to wait to present your product or prototype and see if they will place an order for it. This could be a make-or-break situation with the licensee to go into a deal with you. It may be upsetting to hear if they say that their buyer was not interested and they want to cancel the opportunity altogether. But it's also better to know that you're not going through the motions with them and hear about this later on, after an agreement is signed and they invested in the production and they don't sell anything. In that case, your contract gets terminated, leaving both you and them disappointed. Or maybe they have another buyer that they can show it to and keep the potential deal active, and you'll wait to hear the results of their next meeting and that could work out great!

One of my products went through that routine. One of the buyers said no and we waited until their next buyer meeting and we were good. The buyer loved the product and we moved forward with the deal and the product is in another distribution channel. My licensee and I earn from it. Lessons learned.

Let's make the deal. An agreement can include some or all of these: A royalty rate that's agreed on by you as the licensor and the licensee, the term of the agreement, which is the length of time of the agreement, and the territory, meaning what country or countries it will cover. Also, exclusivity and certain distribution channels, along with minimum guarantees of how many units are expected to sell. Sometimes there are advances against future royalties. A licensee may start off by presenting you with a simple *term sheet* before sending you the full licensing agreement to make sure that you›re both on the same page. This term sheet can include their company and you and your company, royalty rate offered, term, territory, and any advances offered.

Usually, every quarter you would receive a royalty report showing the sell-throughs and the wholesale cost that they sold to their retailers and vendors and what your gross royalties total up. Then there could sometimes be reserves held for returns that you share with the licensee and may be deducted from your side of the payment. Many inventors ask; how do they know? How much do they really sell? You can add a clause in the agreement that you have the right to audit their books once a year and they would have to return the difference and possibly pay some penalty for the inaccuracy. Ultimately you want to have and build trust with the licensee.

Here are some thoughts before making the deal.

Although I'm providing guidance on this subject, some people prefer to use an intellectual property attorney to review the legalities of the agreement. Another thought, should you incorporate as a business entity? Speak with your accountant about the best type of business structure for you, based on your finances and the way you file your tax returns. In my opinion, the time to incorporate is when you enter it into a deal with the licensee. Once you have your corporate structure in place, you can keep track of any investment you put in, like legal fees, prototypes and engineering, as examples. Just keep track of what you spend or have spent as possible tax write- offs. The licensee can also pay you personally, but I prefer a corporation because you never know when someone may challenge product liability or your intellectual property. You want to shield your personal assets from your business side. To open a business bank account, you'll need to show the bank your corporate filing documents so you can cash your royalty checks! You're on your way to finding your licensee or getting ready to make your deal!

Earning royalties can either reap rewards of major income or as an additional income stream for you while you still have your day job or you are working on your next idea. Either way, the goal is to get your product out there for sale and be proud to be an inventor!

Understanding Manufacturing Next Steps

You're ready to begin manufacturing!

You've shared your CAD file or specifications of your invention. You found your factory and they provided a quote on the tooling, if necessary. And you know your production cost per unit, based on a quantity, or that MOQ the minimum or- der quantity. At this time, you should have a draft or finished packaging design and copy complete. This was done with the manufacturer, or you hired a graphic or packaging design- er. You should also have prepared instructions if needed for the packaging, or inserted into the packaging, or maybe it's a manual that needs to be created.

Don't forget about the final touches of your packaging by adding a unique barcode number. If you're going to go in distribution with retailers, then you'll need your own barcode account. You can go to the website GS1US.org. They're the ones that administer those UPC barcodes (Universal Product Code). The barcode itself is encoded with a couple of important things like the country of origin, usually where your company is headquartered, and your company prefix where you're assigned a unique identification number. The first part of the barcode is for the global supply chain to look up a company and the rest is a code for the product you're selling and its description. If you try to sell or purchase barcodes with the third party company, those barcodes are going to have the wrong company prefix. I don't think it's a good idea to work with someone else's prefix. Just get your own. Beyond that, a barcode is an ID that's linked to a product for as long as the barcode system is used. For example, while writing this I am snacking on a jar of mixed nuts from Costco's Kirkland brand. I'm looking at the prefix of the product barcode and it starts with 96619, which is for Kirkland. Then there's a string of numbers afterwards which would relate to the specific product information stored within the universal barcode database. When a retailer rings you up at the register, the barcode information for that product is retrieved and also used for inventory purposes. Interesting. Barcodes.

Once your product is produced or even before it's produced, let's revisit these questions:

Where will you be storing your product? Will you have a warehouse? Do a quick search online for warehouses or storage facilities near your zip code. You can get the box dimensions from the factory or find out how many pallets you have from your production, along with the inner and master carton dimensions to determine the space that you'll need to reserve. There are also those local self-storage units that are reasonably priced and can be convenient or close to your house. Will you hire a fulfillment center that picks, packs, and ships your orders for you? They charge you, instead of you packing and shipping the products yourself and they also charge you for the space you take up in their warehouse. Many of them have software or programs online where you can see your total units available and you can direct them to where to ship and how many units to ship using your carrier's shipping account or theirs. If you plan on using this type of service, be prepared to add this to your operational expenses. You want to make sure you have enough margin to make a good profit from your product and all the effort and money you're investing, or you can ship directly to a retailer's distribution center. If you receive a Purchase Order (PO) from a retailer, they may direct you to ship to their DC, their Distribution Center. You'll have a short window of a date range and time frame when you must schedule your delivery. You must be on time and conform to how they want the packaging, shipping cartons, and labels to their specifications. If you're late or the labels on the boxes are incorrect, you may receive penalties from them which could be costly.

Online retailer programs like Amazon.com allow you to fulfill orders by yourself, the merchant. They have options where you can get notified of orders placed for your product on their site. You print out the packing slip and you can buy discounted shipping from them or you can use your own shipping method, tape the shipping label on the package, and ship out the order. Or they have a program called Fulfillment by Amazon (FBA) where you ship them your inventory directly from your factory or your warehouse to their warehouse and they do everything and charge you additional fees for them to store it in their warehouse. There are advantages to having Amazon hold your inventory. They trust their own systems to ship out your product on time. It's about product placement and building up sales to be known on a site like Amazon.com.

The good thing with Amazon.com or catalog retailers is that you mostly need to focus on the outer packaging for shipping which can allow you to just do your production in bulk with no fancy packaging. Maybe your production of each item just comes to you in a polybag and you can slip it right into the shipping envelope or box.

If you're shipping your product on your own from your direct website or social media campaigns, then perhaps you're making trips to the post office. Or you can set up an account with UPS or FedEx and you can schedule the driver to come to your home or to your office and pick up your shipments.

A few more questions for you and thoughts for setting up your business since you're manufacturing your product.

Did you incorporate your business? Speak with your accountant about the best type of business structure for you based on your finances and how you file your taxes. In my opinion, the best time to incorporate is when you're ready to start receiving money from your sales. Once you have your corporate structure in place, you want to keep track of any investments that you put in, like legal fees, prototypes, and engineering, as examples. Just keep track of what you spend or have spent as possible tax write-offs. You can also run your business as a sole proprietor, but I prefer a corporation because you never know when someone may challenge product liability or your intellectual property. You want to shield your personal assets from your business side. How about setting up a bank account dedicated to your business expenses only. To open a business bank account, you'll need to show the bank your corporate filing documents so you can accept customers' payments!

A few more recommendations about setting up a merchant account to accept credit card payments. You can sign up for a merchant account with your local bank or other popular options, PayPal or Stripe. You'll need your corporate information as well so they can open up a merchant account for you and verify who you are.

Do you have a business phone number? You may want to use your cell phone to start or you can even get a Google voice phone number for free. They assign you a number or you can even pick your own number from what's available. Then you can forward calls to your cell phone or your home phone number and you don't have to give your personal cell phone number. Or you can use a few virtual business phone system routing services from websites like Kall8.com or Grasshopper.com. You can even get a cool local vanity number or toll-free number.

Be proud of where you are and what you've accomplished so far or will very soon with this information. You're on your way to selling your product. You've taken the risks, you're in control and proud to be an inventor!

Marketing for Licensing and Manufacturing Your Invention/Product

How will you get the word out about your invention? One of the best tools you can create yourself is a demo video. Try to keep it less than two minutes long. Here's a word of advice... if you're attempting to license and you want to show a licensee your video, upload and select the unlisted option on YouTube (not public, not private), and only people who receive who receive the link will be able to view that video. Licensees most likely would like to be the first to see something new and may not like that the public can easily view it, especially if they want to be first to the market with your invention. I'm not a big fan of getting too much public exposure when I'm in the middle of trying to find a licensee to do a deal. They'll appreciate that they're one of the first ones to see it and they can be the first ones to show it to their buyers. I also don't suggest doing much on social media or promoting your website, or even having a website when you are attempting to license an invention. After the potential licensee reviews your idea, they sometimes provide feedback that can help you adjust your product design, or what they said can help prepare you for a better pitch or presentation next time. I like to build respect with them and keep my cool if the invention I just pitched gets rejected. This way I leave the door open with them to listen to my next idea.

Smile, and have a good discussion, and be prepared with your potential licensee. Show them your prototype in the video or in person. They'll be able to understand why your invention is for them, and for you to earn royalties and hopefully they feel the same way, as your partner, licensee.

Manufacturing? You want everyone to know about your invention that you are now manufacturing, and buy it! Part of your marketing should be to make a professional video so you can use it for your website and in social media posts, and ad campaigns. I'd prefer not to have everyone see my product before I've had a chance to manufacture it. So, publish it on your website and YouTube, and your social media channels when you're ready to start taking orders. But sometimes people post "coming soon" or "starting to take pre-orders" messages on their website. Both ways can work, your choice. I just like to know I have a product in hand and I have a chance to test it and make sure everything is good before I tell people to order it and it's on its way.

When I'm launching my product, I want everyone to know about it, including industry editors, bloggers, hometown local editors, and local TV stations. You may want to consider hiring a public relations person or company to write a press release for you, or you can write your own press release. Either way, send it to those media outlets and get your story picked up about your new product and about you, the inventor of it! Take the domain you registered and have a website built. Hire someone to run your social media for you, use the account you set up on Upwork to find people to help you with these tasks. Or maybe you can attempt to do it yourself if you're already active on social media. Connect with industry bloggers. Attend tradeshows as both an exhibitor and a visitor. As the manufacturer, it's up to you to get the word out about your product. Start getting the exposure and bringing in the sales. You'll be proud to see people buying and using the product that you created. Remember when it was just an idea in your head?

If you're working on licensing your invention, but this is more on the manufacturing side, you probably created a logo for your brand or product, or both, when you were working on your packaging or when you came up with the name and wanted a logo. Once you have your logo and company name, you can use it on your website, social media, business cards - yes, we still use those. And how about making up some t-shirts, hats, sweatshirts to give to your family, friends and all those that supported you? Be proud of who you are and what you've created!

After you've done all of this work manufacturing your product, what happens next? You can continue to build your brand or expand your product line. Maybe you just want to sell your business and cash out. You might have the intellectual property of a patent and trademark, tooling made and your production set up, and you have a proven track record of sales. Do you like being a serial inventor or entrepreneur? You've proven your concept and maybe you're ready to start on your next business venture. Congratulations and well done!

Or, did you license your invention and now you're earning royalties? Are you ready to work on your next invention? The greatest thing is that you've now gained all this experience and more ideas will begin to flow and you can go through the steps again and again. Going through this journey together navigated us through many different possibilities. I've shown you a process that you can use when you think of all those invention ideas you'll continue to come up with. You'll find you're also able to help others with their ideas now, and when people see your invention and the success you've had, they'll start asking you for help. That's what happened to me! Share your success and be proud to be a successful inventor!

Congrats on Your Success! Thinking Ahead.

You're at a point where you might have hit a single, a double, a triple, or maybe you may have hit a home run with your invention.

Are you going to have residual income, or is your invention going to help you become a millionaire? Or maybe you realized that if you would have gone any further with your first idea you may have spent more time, money, energy and effort on hitting a brick wall, and that's ok, you'll move on to your next ideas with all this knowledge you now have. Or, did you have a great experience going through this journey? Now, you're prepared for when you have your next big idea. Either way, you've learned a great lesson.

The life of an inventor is very interesting. We're always looking at things from a different perspective and the difference with us is that we know how to take action and we now know what to do every time we have that big idea. That's why we're together right now, to help each other get to the next level. So, whether it's this idea or the next one, I'm glad I was part of it with you and I wish you all the best.

Keep on inventing!

Brian Fried

www.ingramcontent.com/pod-product-compliance
Lightning Source LLC
Chambersburg PA
CBHW071842290426
44109CB00017B/1900